www.finishinglinepress.com

New Lebanon

poems by

Elizabeth Poreba

Finishing Line Press
Georgetown, Kentucky

New Lebanon

ACKNOWLEDGMENTS

To the past, present, and future residents of New Lebanon, New York,
including the humans.

"A Large Elm on Route 5" was first published in *Commonweal*, January 1,
2023.

Publisher: Leah Huete de Maines
Editor: Christen Kincaid
Cover Art: Elizabeth Poreba
Author Photo: John Poreba
Cover Design: Elizabeth Maines McCleavy

Order online: www.finishinglinepress.com
also available on amazon.com

Author inquiries and mail orders:
Finishing Line Press
PO Box 1626
Georgetown, Kentucky 40324
USA

Table of Contents

Every place whereon the soles of your feet shall tread shall be yours: from the wilderness and Lebanon, from the river, the river Euphrates, even unto the uttermost sea shall your coast be.

Deuteronomy 11:24

New Lebanon Is a Town in Columbia County, New York

This hilly area, possibly called Pennekoes,
may have been sold to the Van Rensselaer family
by a person understood to be Eskuvius, supposedly
the head Sachem and Peace Chief of the Machicans.

Eskuvius' people lived in various spots along Routes 22 and 20,
following the supply of wood and game as seasons changed,
so he might have thought the sale strange,
and the contract as perplexing to him as the white men
found his signature, a wolf that looked to them
like a "charming ...giraffe with short legs."

"With scarcely an exception their lands were bought,
not stolen. The price was often trifling indeed,
but satisfactory to the owner," wrote Edward Collier,
Doctor of Divinity, in his 1914 book
Kinderhook and Its Indians.

Lucky

Named by Bible believers, a likely place,
too steep for big farms but rich on southern slopes.

Known for the mountain where Shakers danced
and inspired licentious thoughts.

Hills once wooded were soon
vast *rolling gardens* wrote a diarist—

Not New nor Lebanon to the Stockbridge tribe
enticed to town and oblivion.

Now, as rapid as the runoff from its rivers
that never cease despite the season

and lavish themselves among the pines,
nervous history denudes the first Lebanon

and leaves this one intact,
tucked in new growth,

scarcely knowing its luck.

The Bear

You, on spotting the majesty of my haunches,
    see nothing.
You see only a bear, your attention stupidly narrow,
    unlike mine, panoramic, fibrous with charged particles.
If you were a serious witness,
    you would see a rug, moccasins.
You would savor my gristle between your teeth, the taste of my grease,
    my muscles pounded to dry strips, my liver's elixir.
You would feel the heft of my bones fine-tuned to knives,
    my claws around your neck channeling my power to heal.

With you behind me, I have plenty of time to stop at a berry bush, a
    turd,
        a sweet tuft.
You see in my rolling backside only something comic, cunning,
    which a winter of warmth could be providing.

Along the Taconic Overthrust

There is a rock that resembles my grandfather.
It is grey and angular.
The lichen that tops its flat surface is white, like my grandfather's thick hair.
The rock is creased in shades of grey, my grandfather's suits.
Its stripes suggest a history of intense events crosshatched by marble lines, the striations on my grandfather's face.
My grandfather sat as this rock sits, not much to say.
He was a doughboy who fixed typewriters for the Great War.
I knew people who were born two centuries ago.
I can tell you they were quieter then.
Now people cry and hold on to each other as if they are drowning or
    melting,
as if the rain bore them by itself.
Where are the minerals?
I always stop at the rock and bring it a smaller rock,
maybe a lost bit of itself, or shale,
or a granite pebble, a white marble chunk.
Quite a collection on top of the rock by now,
on an extrusion, pointing west like a ship's prow.

Cemetery of the Evergreens, New Lebanon, NY

Looming upon a knoll, a sarcophagus to Samuel J. Tilden,
STILL TRUST THE PEOPLE engraved upon the rim.

Barn Burner, Free Soiler, Abolitionist and opponent of Tammany,
he won a majority, but because the country's slide in '73
(it was agreed) had less to do with the falling price of cotton
than with the foolishness of Black men voting,
Hayes' "self government's blessing" got the win.

Tilden never ran again, never married, left his money to libraries.

STILL he wrote (a weakened man, younger than I am)
THE PEOPLE (nothing lyric, nothing personal),
planning his grand tomb in the midst of this little town
that he'd long since left.

                THE PEOPLE, yes, leaving us this,
this eyesore you might say, landmarked now,
bronze acanthus leaf wreath long since stolen for scrap,
rest for this true believer, high-minded governor,
who grew up among these hills when they were farmed
and fruitful, bristling now with scrawny trees that scarcely cool
the trailer parks and second homes of the town's more fortunate
citizens.

Pileated Woodpecker

Long ago, it had monstrous cousins,
its smallness a useful weapon.
At work now upon a withered sumac
toothless beak prying a snack
from the bleak of a too-warm winter,
my crow-sized neighbor,
red topknot easy to spot,
friendly forest rat-tat-tat,
who knows how to embrace
the swaying branch
and preserve its ancestral crest
from one unsteady state to the next.

Ravine

The bus-sized rock above the brook
is propped and split by a hemlock twice as thick
as I am and higher than a house, its needled fronds
reduced to mist in distance.

Close up, the rock's a pile, puzzle pieces of itself,
a creature's shattered shell,
fractured by a force below,
its fissures lined in lichen, mosaic
of its unmaking.

A mind alert for signs could find,
in this *pas de deux* of rock and tree,
the work of a deep vitality,
and might see, in the blasted birch nearby,
its shattered top bent, another witness,
head tilted in astonishment.

Physics

When the force
          of floods upstream
                    hits rocks
                              and forms arcs,
                                        the brook takes
                              leaps and last night's
                    downpour becomes
          parabolas that match
the tangled raspberry patch
          lining the banks.
                    Look how ferns spring
                              from last year's fronds,
                                        fountains arch back
                              and rockets
                    ease to a curve
          after shooting
up straight.
          What looks free
                    follows paths
                              around fixed points.

A Large Elm on Route 5

You ask what I am, but understand the answer is not subject to form
or rather it is in the form of myself, at this moment
cellulose compounds endlessly recomposing.

I am standing by dint of parts in tension,
for living is motion, ends are beginnings
and hydrogen's cleaving begets all shining.

I am molten, ongoing, shot from the heart
of all making, always giving up
to the gladdening river that is myself.

In the Hall of Birds, Berkshire Museum

They that were songs
a menace to bugs
noisy nestlings
flocks arriving all at once
disturbance in the branches
alive as every idea that once flew

are now pinned to the wall.
The child asks, *Are they real?*

Poverty

Voted Weed of the Week in 2005,
but planted before we knew its reputation,
the Euonymus by the barn has thrived
and repays our complicity in its invasion
by incandescing every fall
into red flame, almost unnatural.

Once each etiolated leaf has burned
brighter than the burnished maple,
it drops with the others in a heap,
and the bush becomes a sum
of branches notched by nubs.

After winter storms, each nub supports
an icy drop, lifting it to the sun,
so that the whole bush becomes
one chandelier charged with light,
not, as in fall, by each leaf's folderol,
but by poverty, holding tight.

Go Out

Go out to the garden and see what's up.

Did those old lettuce seeds grab their chance?
Did the woodchuck leave anything of the spinach
or of the bean shoots heading for the pole?
Has the garlic bent, signaling its readiness?

Go out, though you've done it all before, the sweaty hours
looking for your design beneath spotted spurge, plantain—
how well you've learned the names!

Go out, it's yours, you've given up your ideas
about bearing back baskets, you're ready to settle now—
a stumpy carrot, a few leaves for salad.

Go out to the garden you started. After all,
it's your labor that letting too much grow.
One summer soon, the fence will mark
only a patch of weeds; the next, no fence.

Go out now, see what you can manage.

April

At last, gray and groggy,
A winter of ice in the gutters,
A furnace that hardly warms itself on scarce fuel from suspect sources.
Someone in the wall rustles, someone prefers it inside.
In the front yard, the crab apple leans as if stunned by what's to be
    done.
Enough storing up and shutting down.
The ways that got it through winter must go.
Time to begin the work again.

"Phebe makes a little print..."
—*Emily Dickinson*

Little Brown Bird is the term
for the anonymous ones,
among whose piping this morning
comes a strain so pure,
it moves the morning air
as if from a shining current
at the heart of the planet,
turning to gold its leaden core,
music that could have no form
but this one song, lavished
on my ear, then gone.

Varmints

Two emerge, twin appetites, brindled, dainty nibblers
that could be small rocks, unmoving save for
the action of their ferocious jaws.
Then some calculus tells them
I am too close and they become
matched white spots beneath a bush
leaving me a sense that I am too much,
too large and slow, too covetous of garden,
a blur of noise and confusion,
ignorant of the worth of just living
hand to mouth.

Anything in Motion

There they are again, the Queen Anne's Lace
in sloppy regiments along Route 22, flat-faced,
each filagree disk aloft on a hair-thin stem,
frothy-leaved garden escapees poking up perfect heads
wherever they prefer, the highway department soon
to sheer.
          All for show, this perfectly useless
so-called wild carrot, nothing to harvest,
soon in death bunched into ungainly nests,
but now an exultant pagan crowd
that sways to anything in motion, including
me on my bike, with obscure approbation.

The High Season

A great blue heron summers here,
appearing after the lilacs bloom,
ready to flash from hidden spots
and cast odd shadows on our preoccupations.
We're always pleased when he arrives,
his choice of us a kind of civic boost
since he's free to come and go,
unlike the crows crowding for road kill,
which doesn't interest him, preferring,
as he does, warm amphibian.
Later, he'll be elsewhere, new partner and new nest.
His killer beak preens his shaggy breast.
He need not think of winter yet.

Queechy Lake

The name comes from the Native American Mahican name
Quis-sich-kook, of unknown meaning.
—*Wikipedia*

1.

Children tunneling and heaping sand
to canals moats castles and citadels,
authority alert on her lofty seat,
parents shifting along the thin rim of shade,
the water brimming, our summer city,
our center left by the last glacier,
soft at the shore, unfathomable further out,
thick with tall weeds grazing my belly to the last buoy
where I pause to hear the hum, our buzz of business
unstopped since the first fashioner of birch
who bent a hook for fish, we humans,
always making something.

2.

Parents hover, children touch and scoop, a father flings, the child
        grasps,
terror at the pushing off, small foreshadowing. Elders with veiny legs
ease in to tread, cautious chins up as if for a last look at land.
Some smooth as porpoises slice a seam,
a head emerges, alternate arcs, rest at the rope,
reversal. A white birch leans
overs the scenes and implacable fish
head towards the shallows to be caught and fan patiently in plastic
        buckets.
When he is carried off, he is not the boy he was before.
I want to go to the lake, I want to go to the lake
all the way to the car.

3.

I greet you, aged birches in your white trunks,
presiding as you have all summer,
observing now my last swim of the season.
I direct feet to follow the dip of the beach,
reluctant legs to go deep, hands to sink,
my inner fire to stoke itself
as the chilled silk holds me up,
stern as real life, burning in the coldest spots.
Why are you not amazed?
My courage stuns me, but I'm not much to see,
kicking up a small wake.
Most revered birches, note how the lake
makes me a ripple light as a murmur
before silence to feed your silence, come winter.

New York Fern

You, former fodder for dinosaurs, vestige of towering forests, first
    green life
after great extinction, whose organization of frond and stem can be
    seen pressed
in ancient rocks, now languishing on the north side of my house,
it's another dry day.
Lightning last night brought you nothing but my pity.

Your bracts that crowded profuse in June now brown where they
touch the porch, stick-stemmed in postures that look like misery.

So goes your Order's history of staying still, letting weather work
its will, not venturing flower or seed, impervious to need or loss—

not a strategy available to us.

Weather

This year, the magnolia that usually turns brassy
then heaves its leaves like a hoard of coins
held on, a dull green through November.

When a hard frost seared all that was left
to a drab brown close to black,
the tree shot a few deformed catkins at its crown
like furred antennae tuned to hear
the news of strange changes in the year.

Then snow weighted the leaves and broke some boughs.

Enough remain for green next spring,.
After that, nobody knows.

Autumn Sonnet

The pond on an October night:
summer heat steaming into moonlight,
the sun's work become vapor,
steady smoke offered to stars.

Although the blue heron rarely
landed here, there was life enough.
Deer and hemlock drank their fill,
day lilies bobbed in season
and gave way to golden rod.
Peepers kept up their dialogues,
and children ventured near to hear
the homeward lunge of bullfrogs

who now, like the pond, lie still
and imperturbable.

Seasonal Road Kill

Though the turtle wanted to inch back
to the highway he'd been flung from,
he was rising and falling like a heart,
with a crack that split the perfect pattern
of his dome, and not getting anywhere.
When I found a pail and scooped him in,
he became a stone, the water a faint red,
he who had wanted only to be where
the seasons led.

Found on Route 22

Intact as a saint, preserved
to the least chin whisker,
fawn spots yet flecking the buff
of his foreclosed adulthood,
almost an ordinary kitten except
for the bobcat's blunt tell-tale,
thick pelt not needed now for snow,
ears peaked each side of the space
where cats adore the scratch,
mouth agape showing tiny teeth,
stout legs and ungainly feet.
Only me to mourn the form
that could have roamed
in Shaker Swamp for years to come.

Berkshire Thrift

October over, and now the slow slide to winter, time to hoard
fading embers of the year's colors, which I squandered,
the day drained already to a monotone afternoon, an aimless walk
until I come upon Berkshire Thrift, once derelict,
now a glittering store with pirate costumes, gowns,
capes and wands heaped outside the door.

Free! Take them away! trills the proprietor. *Time for the next holiday!*
and directs me to the Xmas Nook, stuffed with unmatched napkins,
half rolls of wrap and chipped cups, the room vibrating
to a tinny *Silent Night*. Wanting to be polite,
I select a cruet of cheap cut glass cleaned to a high gleam,
reflecting a dream of happy table talk.
"What kind of business plan is this?"
I think. "The cost to heat and light the place, for what?
To sell old stuff for next to nothing?"
Yet feeling in these thoughts some lack,
as if *Love had bade me welcome. Yet my soul drew back.*

italics: George Herbert "Love (iii)"

The Path

I cannot conjure you from a basket,
or traces of sage and thyme on the lawn
or the soft dents of your settlements.
Your memory's as mute as the chert
you plied to soften hide.

Should I pry beneath the highway, I'd find a path
you might have taken along the brook
to the meadow lying east—a swamp now,
the beavers' work. The brook runs
after a good rain, like a refilled vein,
alive despite the loss of all the rest.

Afternoons, the same sun blinds my eyes
where you, too, perhaps, walked west.